Dance

Modern Dance

Andrew Solway

Heinemann Library
Chicago, Illinois

© 2009 Heinemann Library
a division of Pearson Inc.
Chicago, Illinois

Customer Service 888-454-2279
Visit our website at www.heinemannlibrary.com

Editorial: Sarah Shannon and Robyn Hardyman
Design: Steve Mead and Geoff Ward
Picture Research: Maria Joannou
Production: Duncan Gilbert

Originated by Modern Age
Printed and bound by Leo Paper Group

13 12 11 10 09
10 9 8 7 6 5 4 3 2 1

Library of Congress Cataloging-in-Publication Data

Solway, Andrew.
  Modern dance / Andrew Solway.
    p. cm. -- (Dance)
  Includes bibliographical references and index.
  ISBN 978-1-4329-1376-2 (hc)
  1. Modern dance. I. Title.
  GV1783.S67 2008
  792.8--dc22
                        2008014295

Acknowledgments
The publishers would like to thank the following for permission to reproduce photographs:
© Alamy Images p. 31 (Jon Bower London), © Corbis pp. 7 (Robbie Jack), 8 (Historical Picture Archive), 9 (Bettmann), 14 (Sygma/Origlia Franco), 16 (Kipa/David Lefranc), 17 (Hulton-Deutsch Collection), 25 (Sygma/ Thierry Orban), 27 (Viktor Korotayev), 28 (Marco Cristofori), 29 (Kipa/Sergio Gaudenti), 32 (Robbie Jack); © Dee Conway pp. 5, 22, 24, 26, 36, 38, 41, 43; © Getty Images pp. 11 (Time Life Pictures), 13 (Time Life Pictures/ Gjon Mili), 19 (AFP), 20, 40 (Christian Science Monitor); © John Deane p. 4; © Lebrecht Music & Arts pp. 10 (NYPL Performing Arts), 37 (Laurie Lewis); © 2006 TopFoto p. 35 (Alinari).

Cover photograph of Renee Robinson from Alvin Ailey American Dance Theater, reproduced with permission of © Corbis/Julie Lemberger.

Every effort has been made to contact copyright holders of any material reproduced in this book. Any omissions will be rectified in subsequent printings if notice is given to the publishers.

Disclaimer
All the Internet addresses (URLs) given in this book were valid at time of going to press. However, due to the dynamic nature of the Internet, some addresses may have changed, or sites may have changed or ceased to exist since publication. While the author and publishers regret any inconvenience this may cause readers, no responsibility for any such changes can be accepted by either the author or the publishers. It is recommended that adults supervise children on the Internet.

Contents

Some words are printed in bold, **like this.** You can find out what they mean by looking in the glossary, on page 46.

Expression Through Dance

A woman sits on a bench, alone on a stage. Her body is covered by a tube of gray material. Her legs are spread wide, and the material stretches between them. Her arms pull the material down the sides of her face. She moves in sudden convulsions, with pauses in between. The dance suggests some terrible grief.

A man walks into a bleak concrete space carrying a portable CD player. As the music starts, he begins a **"hand jive,"** moving just his arms in stiff gestures. A beat comes into the music, and the man begins to relax— the hand jive becomes large, flowing gestures. Soon he is smiling and his whole body is moving. He is dancing madly around the space, having a wonderful time.

▲ Martha Graham's solo *Lamentation* was a portrait of a grieving woman. Her costume was a tube of fabric that gave her movements more power.

Modern dance pioneers

These are two examples of modern dance. The first is part of *Lamentation*, created in 1930 by Martha Graham. She was one of the **pioneers** of modern dance. The second is from *The Cost of Living*, a dance movie made in 2004 by DV8 Physical Theater. The dances are very different, but they have some things in common. In both cases, the **choreographer** wanted to express something. In *Lamentation* Martha Graham is showing terrible grief through movement, while the dancer in *The Cost of Living* is expressing great joy. In both dances, the choreographers use their own personal style of movement, rather than ballet or some other technique that has set moves and rules.

Modern dance is a kind of performance dance that began nearly 100 years ago. The people who first developed modern dance, and those who later took modern dance in new directions, are not very famous. Most people have not heard of choreographers such as Martha Graham, Merce Cunningham, Pina Bausch, and Mark Morris. However, these dance pioneers, and the dances they made, have had a strong influence on the kinds of dance you see in movies, musicals, and music videos.

▼ Rowan Thorpe of DV8 Physical Theater performs a section from *The Cost of Living* at the Tate Gallery, London, England.

Breakaway from Ballet

Ballet is a very beautiful and powerful form of dancing, but in some ways it is limited. Dancers learn set steps and movements. The arms and legs make large, expressive movements, but the body is much less involved. It is held in position and rarely allowed to relax. Ballet technique makes dancers look light and airy—they rarely connect strongly with the ground. **Choreographers** use ballet's set movements when they make new pieces. The subjects of "classic" (traditional) ballets are mostly fairy tales and legends.

Early in the 20th century, these limitations of ballet were more pronounced than they are today. In both the United States and Europe, there were dancers who wanted to find new ways of moving.

Ballet rebel

In the early 1900s the Ballets Russes (meaning the "Russian Ballet"), led by Serge Diaghilev, was performing glittering, exotic ballets that were popular throughout Europe. The most brilliant dancer in the company was Vaslav Nijinsky. In 1912 Nijinsky began choreographing his own ballets, and in 1913 he choreographed *The Rite of Spring*, a powerful dance piece to music by Igor Stravinsky.

Nijinsky wanted to push ballet beyond dances that were simply beautiful to look at. In *The Rite of Spring,* he had the dancers stamping and bending toward the ground, and the women twisted their bodies into strange positions that suggested grief. Nijinsky also emphasized the effort of the movements, rather than hiding it, as is normal in ballet. Nijinsky's ideas outraged many ballet fans, but these ideas were perhaps the first steps toward modern dance.

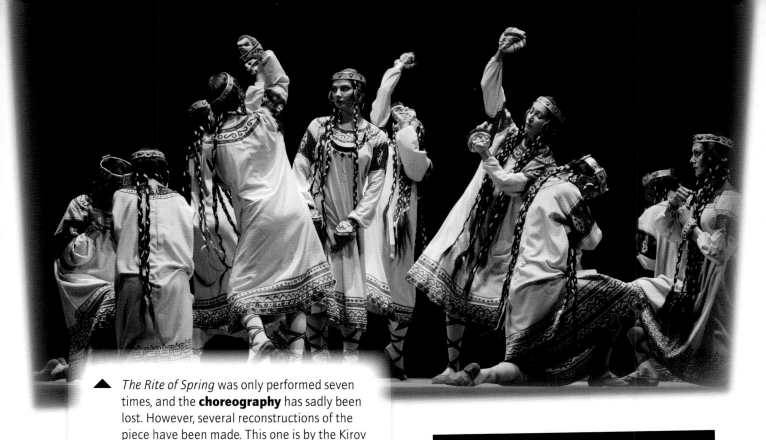

▲ *The Rite of Spring* was only performed seven times, and the **choreography** has sadly been lost. However, several reconstructions of the piece have been made. This one is by the Kirov Ballet of St. Petersburg, Russia.

Freedom in the U.S.

Nijinsky stretched the boundaries of ballet, but three U.S. dancers created styles that were outside ballet altogether. These three sowed the seeds for modern dance.

Loie Fuller began creating her dances in the 1890s. She was at first an actor and singer, but then a **promoter** asked her if she could dance, and she said yes, even though she couldn't! She made a dance called *The Serpentine* in 1891, in which she twisted and moved a dress with a long silk train. Later, she created amazing dances in which she shone colored lights on huge dresses that she manipulated with sticks. Such a combination of dance, costume, and lighting effects had never been seen before, and audiences loved it.

Amazing fact

Riots at the ballet
When *The Rite of Spring* was first performed in Paris in 1913, it caused an uproar. The music, by Igor Stravinsky, was harsh and driving. It was very different from the music ballet audiences were used to. The dancers wore baggy costumes and danced as ballet dancers had never danced before. And the story was a frightening tale of a young girl being **sacrificed** to the god of spring. Some in the audience hated the show. Others thought it was wonderful. The shouting and booing was so loud that the dancers could not hear the music. There were also fights in the audience between those who liked the work and those who did not.

In 1901, when Fuller was at the **Paris Exhibition**, two young U.S. dancers saw her perform. Their names were Isadora Duncan and Ruth St. Denis.

Isadora Duncan had recently moved to Europe and was trying to find audiences for her dancing. Her style was very different from Fuller's. She danced barefoot, in light dresses, and moved with great freedom. Fuller helped Duncan get her first performances in Europe, where she soon became very popular. Duncan's free style of dancing broke away from traditional kinds of dance. It was an inspiration to many dancers who came after her.

▲ This poster from 1893 is an ad for Loie Fuller's performances at the Folies Bergère, a theater in Paris.

Biography

Isadora Duncan

As a child Isadora Duncan lived in San Francisco, California. Her father left home when she was very young, so her mother supported the family by working as a music teacher. Isadora and her sister earned money by teaching dance lessons, but the family was still poor.

Duncan began to invent her own style of dance at an early age. She began to perform in the United States, but audiences did not appreciate her dancing. At the age of about 22 she moved to Europe, and there she found rich **patrons** who encouraged her work. Within a short time she was performing to crowded theaters in all the capitals of Europe. Later, she toured in South America and founded a dance school in Russia, but in her lifetime she was not popular in the United States.

▶ Isadora Duncan is surrounded by her students. The girls who trained with Duncan were nicknamed "Isadorables."

Ruth St. Denis was another dancer who was impressed by Loie Fuller, but she was also inspired by the performance of Japanese dancer Sadi Yaco. St. Denis began to create exotic dances in which she danced like an Egyptian goddess or an Indian princess. Her dances used conventional dance steps, but she moved her arms and body with far more freedom than in other kinds of dance.

By 1914 St. Denis was famous in both the United States and Europe. That year, she met and married a male dancer, Ted Shawn. Together they set up the Denishawn School. This school produced the first truly modern dancers.

Modern Dance Arrives!

In the 1920s, modern dance truly began. The first U.S. modern dance **pioneers** were students at the Denishawn School in Los Angeles. The school taught many forms of movement, including Eastern dance and a kind of free expression movement developed from the work of a Hungarian, Rudolf Laban, and other Europeans.

Angles and contractions

Two of the best dancers at the Denishawn School were Martha Graham and Doris Humphrey. Both taught at the school and performed in the Denishawn Dance Company. After a time, they began to feel dissatisfied with the pieces they were dancing in. They wanted to make a truly new style of dance.

▶ *Soaring* (1922) was one of Doris Humphrey's early dance pieces. Martha Graham danced in some of the early performances of the piece.

Martha Graham she set up her own dance school in 1927. She quickly moved away from the exotic, Eastern style of Denishawn and created her own truly American style of dance.

Most of the dances that Graham made were dramatic. They were usually based around a strong central female character. In her early dances, Graham's movement style was angular. She used flexed feet and bent elbows, and her dancers often showed the effort involved in a movement. This was in strong contrast to the flowing movements and effortless appearance of ballet. Her dancers used their backs more actively than in ballet, with a technique called contraction and release (see technique box).

Technique

Making the back talk

In classical ballet technique, the arms and legs move a great deal, but the back stays fairly straight most of the time. Modern dancers often use the back much more. At the heart of Martha Graham's style was a sudden curving of the back called a contraction. The dancer would contract the back, then straighten or arch it in a movement called the release. Contraction and release could be used to show emotions. Dancers curved their backs in grief or arched them in joy. A contraction could also emphasize a particular movement.

▶ Martha Graham curves her back to create an arc with her long dress, in rehearsal for *Letter to the World*.

Fall and recovery

Doris Humphrey began making her own dances while she was still with Denishawn. In 1928 she left Denishawn along with another dancer, Charles Weidman, to set up a dance company and school.

Doris Humphrey wanted to develop a new way of moving, like Martha Graham. She was interested in a process she called "fall and recovery"—what happened as the body tipped off-balance and began to fall. The kind of movement that she developed flowed more smoothly than Graham's and was less dramatic. She often created **choreography** for groups of dancers, rather than having a central character and supporting dancers, as Graham did.

New expressions

In Germany at about the same time, another style of modern dance was developing. It began with the work of a Hungarian named Rudolf Laban. In 1915 Laban set up a "choreographic institute" in Zurich, Switzerland.

One of Laban's first students was a young woman named Mary Wigman. She was a very good dancer and worked for Laban as his assistant. She began making and performing her own solo dances from 1914, and in 1920 she opened her own dance school in Dresden, Germany. Later, she opened other schools across Europe.

Wigman was interested in making "absolute dances." These were dances that did not tell a story or describe an idea, but were about the movement itself. Often she danced in silence or just to the sound of drumming.

Biography

Ted Shawn
In the 1930s Ted Shawn's marriage to Ruth St. Denis ended, and the Denishawn School closed. Shawn bought a farm in Massachusetts called Jacob's Pillow, and here he formed an all-male dance company. Shawn's Men Dancers performed across the United States until World War II. His dances challenged the prejudice that dancing was only for women. After World War II, Shawn began running a dance festival every summer at Jacob's Pillow. He died in 1972, but the Jacob's Pillow festival still goes on.

A lasting influence

The modern dance pioneers made the world take modern dance seriously. Each of them influenced modern dance in a different way. Martha Graham was probably the most important pioneer. However, the dances of all the pioneers, their teaching, and the things they wrote and said about dance influenced the work of later **choreographers** and dancers.

Biography

Katherine Dunham

Humphrey and Graham were not the only pioneers of modern dance in the United States. In the 1930s, Katherine Dunham began developing a dance style that included movement styles from other cultures. Dunham came from a diverse background. Her father was African-American and her mother was part French-Canadian, part Native American. She studied ballet in her teens, but from early in her dance career she included African-American styles of movement. She traveled in the West Indies, studying the African-style and Latin dances of the Caribbean. When she returned to the United States, she began to choreograph dances that combined U.S. and West Indian dance styles. She choreographed many dances for her own company, and for musicals, **revues**, movies, and opera.

Katherine Dunham often made jazz and social dances into dance pieces for the theater. In this dance, Dunham and her partner, Ohardieno, are doing a dance called the shimmy.

Dance Explosion

In the 1940s and 1950s, modern dance in the United States blossomed. Thousands of people trained in modern dance at the dance schools of Graham, Humphrey, and Dunham. One of Mary Wigman's students, Hanya Holm, opened a dance school that alone had nearly 2,000 students. In Europe, modern dance was not as active. During World War II, all of Wigman's schools were closed down, and Rudolf Laban moved to Great Britain. He worked there with one of his students, Kurt Jooss. Jooss became an important modern dancer and **choreographer**, and in the 1960s he gave Pina Bausch her first opportunity to choreograph (see page 21).

▶ The choreographer Alwin Nikolais uses dancers as one element in a visual spectacle of lights, costumes, and sets. The dancers often hide their individuality behind masks.

Students of the pioneers

By the 1940s, there were many new U.S. dance companies run by dancers who had trained with one of the dance **pioneers**. Many of these companies continued the ideas and principles of their teachers. The Mexican dancer José Limón was a brilliant dancer and choreographer who trained initially with Doris Humphrey. When Humphrey stopped dancing because of **arthritis**, she joined Limón's company as a teacher and choreographer.

Other dancers rejected their teachers' ideas and explored their own ways of moving. Alwin Nikolais trained with Hanya Holm, but his dance work was closer to that of Loie Fuller. Nikolais created a world of fantastic, shifting colors and shapes, using lighting, colored slides, masks, strange costumes, and props. The dancers themselves were anonymous bodies, often with their faces hidden. Anna Sokolow danced with Martha Graham for a time, but she set up her own company in 1936. Sokolow made many angry and sorrowful dances about terrible events such as the **Holocaust**.

Chance dances

One dancer who struck out in his own very different direction was Merce Cunningham. Cunningham joined Martha Graham's dance company in 1939. Graham encouraged him to make his own dance pieces, and he made several for her company. In 1945 he left Graham's company and began to work independently.

From the start of his career, Cunningham made unconventional dances. He worked for many years with the **avant-garde** musician John Cage. Both he and Cage used randomness, or chance, in making dance and music. They would decide things, such as how long a piece would be, by throwing coins. Cunningham and Cage made the dance and the music separately and only brought them together shortly before a performance. In some performances, called "events," Cunningham would mix together sections from different dances, each combined with music that was made for another piece.

Although he works in an unusual way, Cunningham's dances have attracted audiences around the world. He continues to experiment with new ideas even today.

Technique

Skill and character

Merce Cunningham's dance style is complex and very difficult to perform well. His dances involve fast footwork and constant changes of direction. Dancers also need a very flexible back to keep the movements smooth and flowing. His dancers are always strong individuals. Their different characters show in the way they move, and Cunningham often makes **choreography** with particular dancers in mind.

▶ *Ocean* (1994) is a 90-minute dance piece by Merce Cunningham. He used chance processes to put together the 128 dance phrases that make up the piece.

Blues and spirituals

Another important dancer who began to work at this time was Alvin Ailey. Ailey studied with Katherine Dunham and with Los Angeles dancer Lester Horton. In 1954 he moved to New York and started to work on his own dances. His first big success was *Blues Suite*. This dance drew on the pain and anger in African-American blues music. (Blues songs are usually about hard times, bad luck, and troubles.) A year later he made *Revelations*, which quickly became his most popular work. In *Revelations* Ailey used spiritual music that he remembered from his childhood. The words of songs such as "Sinner Man" and "Wade in the Water" gave him inspiration for the dances.

Ailey put together elements from jazz and black dance with modern and ballet techniques to make a dance style that could express powerful emotions but also produce show-stopping theater pieces.

Amazing fact

New experiments

Not all modern dance experiments were a success. Paul Taylor was a dancer with Martha Graham's company in the 1950s. He was looking for a new kind of movement, and he turned to the everyday movements of ordinary people in the city. He put together many of these everyday movements and added his own ideas and music to create a performance called *Seven New Dances*. In one dance, Taylor moved every 10 seconds to the accompaniment of a speaking clock. In another he performed with a dog, and in *Duet* he and another dancer did absolutely nothing for four minutes. Taylor wrote afterward, "It dawns on me that I've been so involved with investigating the exciting world of natural movement that it hasn't occurred to me to imagine how the audience might react." They reacted badly. The newspaper review of one dance critic consisted of the title of the concert with a blank space underneath.

Taylor's experiments were unsuccessful because they were before their time. Many post-modern performances (see page 18) had similarities to *Seven New Dances*.

▼ Dancers rehearse Alvin Ailey's powerful and hugely popular dance piece, *Revelations*.

Post-Modern Dance

By the late 1950s and early 1960s, the modern dance of Graham and Humphrey was no longer new. It had become "traditional" modern dance. A group of young U.S. dancers rejected this tradition and began to ask new questions about dance. The style they developed led to a new movement: post-modern dance. It was called "post-modern" because the dancers saw themselves as moving beyond modern dance, rejecting the ideas and conventions of Martha Graham and other modern dance **pioneers**.

Technique

Improvisation

Dance improvisation is making up movement as you go along. This does not mean that the dancers do anything they want. Often an improvisation will be based around an idea, an emotion, or a set of rules. One dancer might be asked to "move across the space without touching anyone," while another dancer might be told, "Get in the way of anyone moving across the space." Some dancers, such as the U.S. dancer Dana Reitz, use improvisation in performances. Others use it as a way of finding new ideas.

West and east coasts

Post-modern dance began with discussions and workshops on opposite sides of the United States. In San Francisco in the late 1950s, the dancer and teacher Anna Halprin began the Dancers' Workshop. Halprin was interested in **improvisation**—dance that is not set, but rather is invented on the spot. Halprin worked on her ideas with a group of other dancers, musicians, and artists. The use of improvisation in performances was a new idea in modern dance.

Meanwhile in New York, a class in **choreography** at the Cunningham dance studios began producing startling results. The classes were taught by a musician named Robert Dunn. He had worked on music ideas with John Cage. Some of the students in his class also included dancers who had worked with Halprin in San Francisco.

Dance can be anything

Robert Dunn encouraged the students to discuss ideas, try things out, and not judge dances as good or bad. They tried out all kinds of unusual ideas. They accepted any kind of movement as dance. They made dances in which they literally swept the floor, or walked around, or washed the dishes. One of the dancers, Steve Paxton, made a piece in which a large group of people of all ages walk diagonally across the stage. Each person stands or sits down at various points along the way.

▲ *The Miraculous Mandarin* is a dance piece by Lucinda Childs to ballet music originally written by composer Béla Bartók in the 1920s. Childs was a post-modern **choreographer** in the 1960s. Her dances were cool and minimal, using simple movements such as walking and turning.

The discussions and interactions in Dunn's classes, and the excitement of finding new ways to think about dance, led to a great burst of creativity. It was the start of post-modern dance.

Judson Church

In 1962 dancers from Robert Dunn's class organized a performance at the Judson Church in New York. For the next 14 years or so, post-modern dancers regularly performed at the church. This loose group of dancers became known as the Judson Church Dance Theater.

Some of the dances at Judson Church were improvised. In 1970 nine of the dancers formed an improvisation group called the Grand Union. In their performances, Grand Union used snippets of set movement, speaking, lights, games, gestures, and all kinds of props—in fact, anything and everything. Grand Union performances probably included some of the best (and perhaps also some of the worst) moments in post-modern dance.

Post-modern style

Like other modern dancers before them, post-modernists were interested in finding new ways to move. One way they did this was to work with props and equipment. Dancers were given tasks to carry out with the equipment. Trisha Brown, for instance, made several equipment pieces. In the piece *Floor of the Forest*, the dancers worked in a net, several feet off the ground, that had pieces of clothing threaded into it. The dancers wriggled in and out of the clothing. At some performances, a rummage sale took place below while the dance was being performed.

It was not just movement styles that post-modern dancers wanted to challenge. They also experimented with the way in which an audience experiences a performance. One idea they explored was to perform in different kinds of places. Dancer and musician Meredith Monk made the piece *Juice* for performance in three very unusual venues: the first section was in the Guggenheim Museum in New York; the second was in a small theater; and the third was in Monk's loft studio. As the venue changed from a huge museum to a small studio, the audience and the dancers got farther apart, rather than closer together. In the museum, the audience could stand close enough to the dancers to feel their breath. In the theater, the dancers were on a stage, and in the loft they were only present on a video.

▼ This recent performance of Trisha Brown's piece *Floor of the Forest* (1970) was one of several Brown pieces performed by dance students at Documenta 12, an arts festival in Kassel, Germany.

What did post-modernism achieve?

Post-modern dance was short-lived, because it was a period of rebellion against old ideas and experimentation without rules. After a time the post-modern pioneers began to find their own personal styles and went in different ways. For example, the contact improvisation style that Steve Paxton invented has been developed by Paxton and many other dancers worldwide. Although pure post-modern dance has not really survived, the style has had important effects on modern dance as a whole. Because of the experiments of post-modern dancers, choreographers today have a far wider range of movements to work from. Everyday movements, improvisation, unusual locations, and truly relaxed styles are all tools available for today's choreographers.

Technique

Release and contact
Post-modern dancers developed dance techniques in which the body stayed relaxed as it moved. One kind of relaxed movement was called release technique. Dancers worked from inside their bodies rather than looking at the shapes they made in space. They might imagine movement rippling through their body like water or zipping through the body like an electric current.

In contact improvisation, two or more dancers moved while continually in contact with each other. Often each dancer would take part of the other person's weight as they balanced on one another's backs or sank to the ground. Release and contact styles drew on movement ideas from outside dance, such as **Tai Chi** and **martial arts**.

Spreading and Mixing

By the mid-1970s, post-modernism in the United States was running out of steam. Post-modern **pioneers** such as Yvonne Rainer, Trisha Brown, David Gordon, and Steve Paxton were no longer performing together at the Judson Church, but were working separately on their own dance ideas.

Although the first burst of creativity and experimentation had died down, post-modernism did not disappear altogether. Post-modern **choreographers** such as Trisha Brown and Lucinda Childs set up their own companies. They drew on post-modern techniques such as release and contact **improvisation**, but they performed in theaters and used highly trained dancers. Modern dancers began to include elements of post-modern techniques in their training. This affected the style of modern dance, which began to include relaxed movement, sharing weight, and a kind of movement that ripples through the body in a similar way to break-dancing.

◀ *D'un Soir un Jour* is a dance piece by Rosas, the company of Belgian choreographer Anna Therese de Keersmaeker. De Keersmaeker has been influenced by the minimalist dance of Lucinda Childs (see page 19) and by Pina Bausch's work.

Dance outside the U.S.

By the 1970s, people were studying modern dance around the world. Dance companies sprang up in many countries. In the 1980s, some of these companies became internationally famous.

Czech chorographer Jirí Kylián and British choreographer Siobhan Davies both made dances in which movement was the focus of the piece, not a story or a dramatic idea. Kylián led the Netherlands Dance Company. Siobhan Davies created **choreography** for several groups, including her own dance company. Music was important for both dancers. Kylián was trained as a ballet dancer at the Royal Ballet School in London, but his dances are modern rather than **balletic**.

The work of choreographers Édouard Lock of Canada and Wim Vandekeybus of Belgium is very physical and involves challenges and risks for the dancers. In the 1980s, Lock choreographed high-energy duets and group pieces for his group La La La Human Steps. The dancers hurled themselves around the stage in ultra-fast duets to rock music, often with films showing in the background. The dances of Vandekeybus were often about anger and conflict between people, and he also used film in his work.

Some countries have their own strong dance traditions. In Spain, for example, flamenco has remained more important than either ballet or modern dance. In the 1970s, Antonio Gades set up a dance company in which he mixed modern and classical dance ideas with flamenco. In the 1980s, he made a series of movies with director Carlos Saura, such as *Blood Wedding*, which made his style internationally famous.

Biography

Twyla Tharp

Twyla Tharp's early dances were experimental post-modern pieces, and she was part of the Judson Church Dance Theater. However, she moved away from post-modernism in the 1970s. Her dances combined jazz dance, pop music, throwaway gestures, and a sense of fun. In 1973 she was asked to make a dance piece for the Joffrey Ballet in Chicago. The piece she made was hugely popular, and the ballet dancers enjoyed performing in her jazzy, relaxed style. Since that time, she has made pieces for many ballet companies. Her style works for ballet companies because she was trained in ballet herself.

U.S. stars

U.S. dance in the 1980s was full of energy. Molissa Fenley developed high-energy, technical dance; Stephen Petronio made dances about accidents and near-death situations; and Bill T. Jones and Arnie Zane made often-angry dances about subjects such as racism, social injustice, and **censorship**. But the most important dancer to come out of this period was Mark Morris.

Dance facts

Dances for all ages

For over 20 years, the Netherlands Dance Theater (NDT) ran three different dance groups. NDT I was the usual kind of professional dance group. NDT II was a group of young dancers who were 17 to 22 years old. NDT III was a company for dancers over 40. Each company had different dance pieces choreographed for it. Some of the most interesting pieces were for the older dancers, who were strong characters and had great theatrical skills. NDT III was closed down in 2006, but the older dancers do make occasional appearances.

Amazing fact

Dance of darkness

Another kind of modern dance was developed in Japan by Tatsumi Hijikata. The style is called butoh, which is short for Ankoku Butoh ("dance of darkness"). Hijikata developed butoh in the 1960s. The dance was shocking and expressed dark emotions such as anger and despair. It rejected Western ideas of dance, but it also drew on the dance techniques of Mary Wigman. In the 1980s, the dance company Sankai Juku, led by Ushio Amagatsu, developed a very beautiful, magical style of butoh that became popular in Western countries.

▲ *The Egg Stands Out of Curiosity* was created by Ushio Amagatsu, founder of the butoh dance group Sankai Juku.

Mark Morris mixed together material from different kinds of dance and came up with a style that is completely his own. When he was young, he studied folk dance, flamenco, and ballet as well as modern dance. He worked with several modern dance groups, and at the age of 24 began his own dance company. Morris's style is hard to pin down because his work is so wide ranging. He has made dances to **Baroque** music that can look almost like ballet, in addition to very funny, almost slapstick pieces. He has even choreographed a solo for a radio-controlled truck! However, all these different dances are brilliantly made. In the 1980s, he became one of the leading modern dance choreographers in the world.

▼ *Mozart Dances* is a full-evening dance piece by Mark Morris to music by Mozart, with sets by artist Howard Hodgkin. The piece is by turns funny, tender, sad, romantic, and joyous.

Modern Dance Today

Today, it is often difficult to separate modern dance from ballet. Modern dancers often overlap with the ballet world. **Choreographers** such as Twyla Tharp, Mark Morris, and the English choreographer Wayne McGregor often make dances for ballet companies. The modern dancer Matthew Bourne has made an updated version of the classical ballet *Swan Lake*. Ballet choreographers have also crossed over into modern dance territory. William Forsythe is an important ballet choreographer, but he draws heavily on modern ideas and his work has a very modern feel.

From Tai Chi to circus

Today's dancers draw on a huge range of different kinds of movement. Their dance may include movements from many styles of dance, as well as other types of movement such as **martial arts** and circus skills. The British-Asian dancer Akram Khan, for example, is trained in both **kathak** dancing and modern dance. He uses both of these kinds of movement in his **choreography**. Compagnie Montalvo-Hervieu, from France, uses a combination of modern, African dance, and break-dancing in its shows. Other choreographers use movement from outside dance. For instance, the Cloud Gate Dance Theater in Taiwan uses **meditation**, martial arts, and **Tai Chi** in its work.

◀ Akram Khan is trained both as a modern dancer and as an Indian kathak dancer. He has used this mix of cultures to create his own unique dance style.

26

▶ In their performances, the Brazilian company De La Guarda combines exciting aerial movement, live music, audience participation, and dramatic theatrical effects like this cascade of water.

Dance companies today can draw on a wider range of other media than at any time in the past. Wayne McGregor relies on film, lighting, and design as much as on dance. Brazilian Deborah Colker's dances are often focused on a large set piece, such as the 23-foot (7-meter) wheel that takes up the center of the stage in *Roto*. The dancers move on and off the wheel, which swings and spins as they do so.

Modern dancers today use all kinds of movement, perform in many different spaces, and use many kinds of media in their work. What connects all these dances together is a love of moving and a desire to express something—an idea or something less clear cut such as an emotion—through movement.

Dance facts

Pop and modern

Many of today's top modern choreographers make dances for music videos as well as for the stage. For example, both Akram Khan and the new British choreographer Rafael Bonachela have made videos with pop singer Kylie Minogue.

Amazing fact

Computerized dancers

Some choreographers have experimented with computer-generated dancers in their performances. In Merce Cunningham's piece *Biped*, for example, computer-generated "stick people" shared the stage with real dancers. The movement of the stick figures was very realistic because it was created using a process called "motion capture," in which the movements of a real dancer are computerized. Cunningham has also helped to develop the computer software DanceForms (see page 42).

Made for Performance

If you go dancing at a club or do some salsa or folk dancing, you are doing it for fun. Unless you enter a dance competition, you are not expecting other people to watch. However, modern dance is made for an audience. Dances made for performing need to be different from dancing for fun.

Stagecraft

Dances made for an audience have to be organized. It is pointless to display superb movement if an audience cannot see it. Most modern dance is made for a stage. It is designed to be seen from one side (the front of the stage). The most important action should happen in the center of the stage, because this is the most "powerful" part of the performance space, where the audience naturally looks. Dancers have to be arranged so that they do not block each other, and if there are patterns in the way the dancers move, they have to be clear from the front.

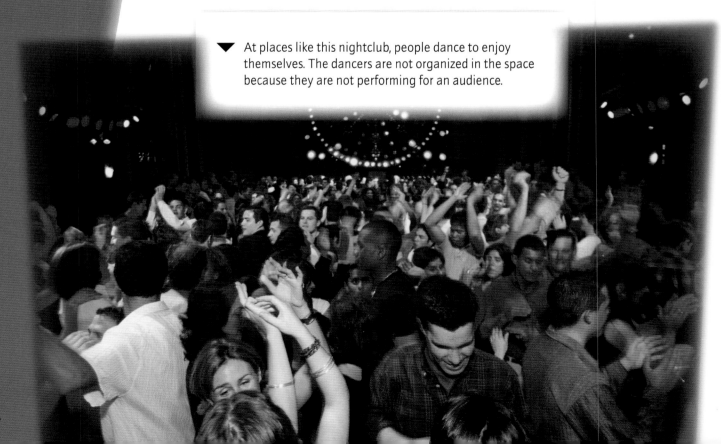

▼ At places like this nightclub, people dance to enjoy themselves. The dancers are not organized in the space because they are not performing for an audience.

28

▲ Pina Bausch often breaks stage rules. In her piece *Die Fensterputzer* (*The Window-Cleaner*), the 16-foot (5-meter) hill of red silk flowers is stunning but difficult to dance on. Dancers block each other, talk at the same time, or do things in corners where we cannot see. Yet the overall result is a gripping performance.

In many folk or ballroom dances, the dance patterns are repeated all the way through the dance. A dance for performance usually needs some variety through time, to keep the audience interested. For example, a dance may start quickly, slow down, then speed up again, or may begin slow and quiet, then gradually build to a climax. **Choreographers** often repeat movements several times in a dance, so that the audience begins to recognize the movements. This helps to tie the dance together as a unified piece. There is usually also one main piece of dancing going on, so that the audience knows where to focus its attention.

Great choreographers often break dance performance "rules." For example, in some Merce Cunningham pieces, the set blocks the audience's view of some of the dance. However, the way that the movement appears and disappears becomes an important quality of the piece. Pina Bausch often has several different things happening on stage at once, so that it is impossible to watch everything that is happening. This gives the audience a sense of involvement and choice: if it loses interest in one part of the action, it can focus on another.

Different spaces

Modern dance has never been limited just to theater spaces. Isadora Duncan often danced outdoors, and Rudolf Laban's Movement Choirs often involved large numbers of people performing outside. In the 1960s, post-modern dancers performed in many non-dance spaces, ranging from the Guggenheim Museum to a boating lake. In Trisha Brown's *Roof Piece*, the dancers were spread out on the roofs of several buildings in the SoHo district of New York.

Many dancers since the 1960s have performed outside the theater. Sometimes the pieces are site-specific. This means that they are made to be performed in a particular place. Canadian choreographer Noémie Lafrance has been making site-specific dances since 2001. *Descent* was made for performance in a stairwell. *Noir* took place in a multi-story parking lot, with the audience sitting in cars. The car headlights were the lighting for the show.

Amazing fact

Moving the audience

Dancer Douglas Dunn broke almost all the rules of theater in his 1974 work *101*. For four hours each day, six days a week, for seven weeks, he laid motionless on top of a maze he had built in his New York dance studio. In this dance piece the audience did all the moving. If people wanted to see Dunn, they had to scramble through the wooden maze that filled the entire loft to the top, where he lay completely still.

Technique

Rules of the stage

In her book *The Art of Making Dances*, Doris Humphrey explains how being in different parts of the stage affects the dancing that happens there. At the back of the stage, the dancer is someone "remote, impersonal, who we do not know." As the dancer moves toward the center of the stage, he or she grows in strength and power. However, if the dancer moves beyond the center and down to the front, he or she becomes more ordinary—"a friend, someone we care about." Humphrey also explains why choreographers do not make whole dances in the center of the stage: "After a short while [in the center], the power begins to fade, as though the electricity had failed . . . the magic of the center is gone."

Dance facts

Dance with a backhoe

Transports Exceptionnels, choreographed by French dancer Dominique Boivin, is a duet for a dancer and a mechanical backhoe. The idea sounds like a joke or a gimmick, but in fact the dance is surprisingly beautiful. Boivin said about the dance: "I imagine the machine as a human . . . like Boris Karloff in the film *Frankenstein*. In its power, elegance, and beauty, the machine can remind us of the world of industry."

▲ Dancer Pascale Houbin duets with a backhoe in *Transports Exceptionnels*.

How to Make a Dance

Different **choreographers** make dances in different ways. However, we can look at some of the work that goes into making a dance piece.

Making and developing movement

Most choreographers have something that they want to get across in a dance. They may want to tell a story, express their feelings about something, or be inspired by a painting or a poem. Martha Graham's dance *Letter to the World* was inspired by the poetry of Emily Dickinson. They may be inspired by something **abstract**, such as a movement idea. Siobhan Davies usually starts her pieces from movement ideas.

The next step is often to make movement phrases. These are short sequences of movements that connect together. Not all choreographers make up all the movements themselves. Pina Bausch often asks her dancers to try **improvisation** around an idea or a task. She watches them, then picks material that fits with the overall theme of the dance.

▼ In this image from the dance *Elsa Canasta* by choreographer Javier De Frutos, the positions of the three women lead the eye toward the male dancer, who is "reaching for the sky." The whole image has a sense of yearning.

To make a dance of a reasonable length, each movement phrase needs to be "stretched out." Choreographers may make variations by adding traveling steps, jumps, or turns, by doing it backward, or by speeding some parts up and slowing other parts down.

In group pieces, there are many other ways of developing and arranging movement phrases. Two dancers could perform different phrases at the same time or the same phrase at different times. This is called moving in **canon**. Groups of dancers can do the same phrase in different places, or in different groupings, or facing different ways.

Putting the pieces together

The choreographer also needs an overall structure for the dance, so the audience can make sense of the piece. Some choreographers do not plan this structure in advance. They let it grow naturally, with one section following on from another. Sometimes the structure may come from the idea behind the dance, such as the story, or from the music.

Dance facts

Making *Set and Reset*

When Trisha Brown made her dance *Set and Reset* in 1983, she started with a long movement phrase that went around the outside of the space. She taught the phrase to her dancers, then asked them to improvise with it, using the following set of rules:

1. Keep it simple.
2. Play with visibility and invisibility.
3. If you don't know what to do, get in line.
4. Stay on the outside edge of the stage.
5. Act on instinct.

While she was making the dance, Brown worked closely with Laurie Anderson, who was writing the music. Every time a new section of the dance was finished, Brown would send a video of it to Anderson. Anderson would start mixing together music ideas as she watched the video on screen. *Set and Reset* is one of Brown's most popular pieces.

Sometimes a choreographer creates a more formal structure using different sections of movement. If they have three sections, for instance (sections A, B, and C), one structure could be to go through all three sections then back to the beginning—ABCA. Often the A section is changed a bit the second time it happens. Or one section can be used as a sort of "chorus"—ABACAD, and so on. A third kind of structure is an accumulation. This means the dancer does movement A, then AB, then ABC, then ABCD, and so on.

Music and Sound

Most classical ballet pieces are danced to the music of 19th-century composers such as Tchaikovsky and Chopin. In the 1920s, the modern dance **pioneers** broke with this tradition. Doris Humphrey created *Water Study* to be danced in silence, and Mary Wigman used silence or drumming to accompany her dances. In *Letter to the World,* Martha Graham used an actor speaking Emily Dickinson's poetry in the dance piece. Since that time, modern dancers have continued to look for new ways to use music and sound with their dances.

Changes in music

Until the 1950s, most modern dancers used classical music with their dance pieces. However, there were some exceptions. Katherine Dunham, for example, created **choreography** based on jazz and Caribbean music.

When post-modern dancers began to experiment with dance in the 1960s, they experimented with music and sound, too. Some dancers used popular music as a soundtrack. Twyla Tharp, for example, used pop music such as the Beach Boys for several dances. Others used different kinds of sounds. Steve Paxton made a dance using eight transistor radios, while many dancers used tapes of people reading or of everyday sounds. In one dance called *Yellowbelly*, Trisha Brown got the audience to shout "yellowbelly!" at her while she danced.

Dance facts

Do it yourself

Sometimes dancers make their own music. In Twyla Tharp's dance *Fugue*, for example, the dancers stamp and tap on the floor to make a rhythmic soundtrack to their movements. Meredith Monk often uses performers who can both sing and move at the same time. It is also possible to use technology to make music as you move. Infra-red light beams are shone across the stage, and every time a dancer's body moves through one of these beams, it triggers a sound. The sound can be anything from a clang to a whole phrase of music.

▼ Meredith Monk is a singer and composer as well as a choreographer. Often she calls her performances "operas."

Together or apart

Since the 1960s, modern dancers have used just about every kind of music possible. Some dancers work with musicians playing live, while others use recorded music or electronics.

Some **choreographers** make dance that is strongly linked to the music. Mark Morris studies the score of the music he is working with, and this is the starting point for the dance. Merce Cunningham uses music in a completely different way—the dance and music are made entirely separately. Other choreographers fall between these two extremes of connection between music and dance.

Sets, Costumes, Lighting

Most dances made for performance have costumes, some kind of set, and lighting. These can all play an important part in a dance piece.

A lot from a little

Early modern dances used sets and costumes in a limited way, often because they had no money for anything more elaborate. However, these simple sets and costumes could be very effective. In Doris Humphrey's piece *Soaring*, a large square of silk acts as a constantly changing set for the dance. The sculptor Isamu Noguchi made sets for many Martha Graham pieces. His powerful sculptures could suggest a whole setting very simply. For *Frontier*, for instance, Noguchi's set was a section of fencing center stage, with a white rope running diagonally upward on either side.

Some dances are built around very simple props or costumes. The tube of stretchy material that Martha Graham wore for the dance *Lamentation* was an essential part of the piece (see page 4). Without the tube, the movement simply would not work. David Gordon has built many dances around another prop—a folding metal chair. Many **choreographers** have made dances using chairs, but no other choreographer has so fully explored the possibilities of this simple prop.

▲ The white scaffolding at the center of Glen Tetley's *Pierrot Lunaire* is an integral part of the dance piece.

Multimedia mix

Surfing on the Short Waves by U.S. choreographer Timothy Buckley was a truly multimedia dance piece. Buckley improvised on stage with British comic Philip Herbert. Around the performers were banks of TV screens. Some screens showed dances filmed earlier. Others showed live footage filmed by three cameramen. One screen might show just the arms of the performers, while another showed them filmed from floor level. Added to all this was music by Blue Gene Tyranny, playing keyboards and synthesizer.

▲ Klaus Obermeier is a multimedia artist who uses computerized images in unusual ways. In this version of Stravinski's *Rite of Spring*, the dancer seems to float above the orchestra.

Using technology

In the 1950s, Alwin Nikolais was one of the first dancers to really see the possibilities of using technology in dance. His performances were always pushing the boundaries of what it was possible to do with lighting, sound, props, and costumes. In the 1960s, post-modern choreographers experimented with using film in their work. Yvonne Rainer began using pieces of film in her work in 1968, and later moved away from dance and into filmmaking. Trisha Brown made a dance in which she performed a solo called *Homemade* wearing a film projector on her back. The projector showed a film of Brown doing the same dance.

By the 1990s, dancers had many more kinds of technology available. Choreographer Wayne McGregor and his company Random Dance exploit all kinds of technology in their dances. Animation, digital film, electronic sound, and virtual dancers are all used alongside the live **choreography**.

Teaching and Learning

Learning modern dance is like training for a sport, learning a musical instrument, and learning to act, all at the same time. The body has to develop a wide range of movement and to be skilled at learning and performing complex movement. A top dancer needs to train as hard as a top athlete. However, a dancer also needs to be creative, to express ideas and emotions through movement, and to understand how to perform for an audience.

Strong and flexible

A dancer's body has to be flexible. Modern dance involves a wide range of movement in the legs and arms. Dancers also need a flexible back, so that movements can pass through the body rather than happening just in the limbs.

Modern dancers also have to be strong. They need strong legs for jumps and pliés (leg bends), and a strong stomach and back for leg lifts, kicks, and floor work. Unlike male ballet dancers, they do not usually have to lift other dancers straight into the air. Lifts in modern dance are often more complex, involving coordination and timing more than strength.

▶ In this lift from Shobana Jeyasingh's dance *Flicker*, the women jump onto the men's hands rather than being directly lifted.

Dancers also need speed, coordination, and balance. They have to perform skilled movements such as turns, balances, and complex step patterns. A great deal of dance training involves repeating movements again and again in order to develop these skills.

Movement quality

The quality of dancers' movement is just as important as what they can do. Merce Cunningham continued to dance when he had a limited range of movement and suffered from **arthritis**. However, the quality and variety of his movement made him fascinating to watch, even at an advanced age.

Dance teachers often use images to help improve movement quality. For instance, they might tell students to imagine movement flowing through the body like water or a movement bursting from the center like an explosion. If dancers are trained to use ideas and their imagination, these images can have real physical effects.

Dance schools

Because there is so much to learn, teaching has always been important in modern dance. Great **choreographers** such as Graham, Humphrey, Cunningham, Alvin Ailey, Trisha Brown, and Mark Morris have set up full-time dance schools, where students can learn their dance technique. Other dance programs in colleges do not focus on one particular technique.

Technique

A modern dance class
There are many different kinds of dance technique class. However, most modern dance classes will include the following sections:

- Warm-up exercises to ease the body into movement without causing damage to muscles and joints.
- Simple technical exercises isolating particular elements of a technique, such as work on legs or torso or practicing balance or coordination.
- Work across the floor, often with simple step combinations.
- One or more dance phrases, to put together various techniques practiced in class and to improve the dancer's ability to remember movement sequences.
- Stretching and warm-down exercises, to help minimize stiffness after class and to improve the dancer's range of movement.

▲ Most professional dance companies do workshops and classes in schools. In this workshop, students are learning elements of the Alvin Ailey dance *Revelations*.

Today, dance schools train dancers using a wide range of techniques. Students may learn **Tai Chi** or **Pilates** for good posture and to help the basic quality of their movement. They may learn ballet for strength and speed, especially in the legs. They may learn Graham or other modern dance techniques for developing body strength and flexibility and to learn skills such as floor work (movements sitting, kneeling, or lying on the floor). And they may learn release techniques (see page 21) in order to move with relaxation and ease.

In addition to all the technical training, dance schools teach students about **choreography.** This involves learning how to structure dances, how to work with groups, and how to use **improvisation** as a way of developing movement. Students also learn about the work of other dancers and about other arts such as music, painting, and sculpture.

Classes and workshops

Not everyone who enjoys moving wants to become a professional dancer, and not all dancers run dance schools. Many people learn to dance in classes and workshops. Some dancers teach classes in community centers and church halls that are open to anyone. Others go into schools to teach young people. They may combine classes with demonstrations or workshops on choreography. Dancers may also teach in other places, such as prisons, hospitals, and places for people with **special needs**. Dance has been used as a physical **therapy** for many years. Dance training can make huge improvements in the movement skills of some people with physical difficulties. It can also help people with disorders such as **autism**.

Dance facts

Set and Reset/Reset

The Trisha Brown Dance Company has developed a teaching project for dance schools known as Set and Reset/Reset. Dance teachers who know Trisha Brown's piece *Set and Reset* teach the basic dance material to a group of students. The students then work with the teacher to develop their own version of the dance, using the same rules that Brown gave to her dancers when she originally made up the piece (see page 33).

▼ CandoCo is a British modern dance group of disabled and non-disabled dancers. *Sunbyrne*, by U.S. choreographer Doug Elkins, is a joyful mix of movement ranging from break-dance to hula hooping.

The Dance of Tomorrow?

In one sense, modern dance is not "modern" anymore. Dance forms such as break-dance and hip-hop are far newer than the dances of Martha Graham and Doris Humphrey. However, modern dance renews itself all the time. New dancers and **choreographers** are not satisfied with the dances and dance techniques that already exist. They want to strike out into new territory and make dances that are relevant for today. So, what changes might happen in modern dance in the future?

Preserving traditions

One thing that becomes more and more important as modern dance grows older is to preserve the dances of the past. Many dance companies regularly revive dances from the past. The Alvin Ailey Company has recreated dances by Katherine Dunham and Ted Shawn, and the Martha Graham Company preserves Graham's works. To revive a dance properly you need a video of the dance for an overall impression, written notation to preserve all the details, and, if possible, someone who danced in it to supply the kind of information about feeling and quality that is lost in video and notation.

Technique

DanceForms

DanceForms is a kind of computer animation software that can be used for choreographing and recording dances. A dancer or choreographer can make animated figures and control their movements. The program can be used to record pieces of dance or to try out new movements. It is even possible to program figures to do whole sequences and then project them onto a screen as part of a dance piece.

▲ Choreographer Shobana Jeyasingh combines ideas from different cultures and is always experimenting. Her dance piece *Surface Tension* combines dance techniques from Europe and India with electronic music from South Africa.

Variety and technology

As modern dance has become more international, it has drawn on ideas from a greater variety of sources. This expanding influence is likely to widen in the future. Choreographers might combine modern dance with several other kinds of dance and movement. What might emerge from, for example, a mix of modern dance, salsa, and synchronized swimming?

More and more choreographers are likely to use technology in their dances, even when they are creating **choreography**. Today's computer animation programs are so powerful and realistic that it is possible to use them to choreograph movement on screen. The software DanceForms can already be used this way. In the future, more choreographers will create on-screen dancers and use them in performances. It may even become possible to use holographic dancers to move through space in three dimensions.

However modern dance changes in the future, it will still need creative choreographers and dancers to explore new movement and go in new directions. Who knows—in a few years, *you* might be the future of modern dance.

Modern Dance Factfile

Ailey, Alvin (U.S.), 1931–1989. African-American **choreographer**. Founded one of the most popular and successful of all modern dance companies. *Revelations* (1960).

Bausch, Pina (German), b. 1940. Creator of many important dance-theater pieces, from *Wind of Time* (1969) to *Vollmond* (2006).

Bourne, Matthew (British), b. 1960. Modern dance-maker, originally made short, witty dance pieces but went on to make new versions of ballets and movies such as *Swan Lake* (1995) and *Edward Scissorhands* (2005).

Brown, Trisha (U.S.), b. 1936. Post-modern choreographer and internationally successful dance-maker. *Accumulation* (1971), *Water Motor* (1978), *Set and Reset* (1983), *L'Orfeo* (1998).

Bruce, Christopher (British), b. 1945. One of Great Britain's most important modern choreographers. His dramatic **choreography** often tells a story. *Cruel Garden* (1977), *Ghost Dances* (1981), *The Dream Is Over* (1986), *God's Plenty* (1999).

Clark, Michael (British), b. 1962. Choreographer who began by aiming to make shocking and outrageous dances, but went on to become an important dance-maker. *I Am Curious Orange* (1988), *Wrong Wrong* (with Steve Petronio 1991), *O* (1994), *Mmm* (2006).

Colker, Deborah (Brazilian), b. 1961. Choreographer who combines athletic dance with impressive stage sets such as a large wheel and a three-story house. *Rota* (1997), *Casa* (1999), *Knot* (2005).

Cunningham, Merce (U.S.), b. 1919. One of the greatest modern dance-makers. Uses randomness and chance in his work, one of the first to use computerized dancers. *Summerspace* (1958), *Rainforest* (1968), *Field and Figures* (1989), *Biped* (1999).

Davies, Siobhan (British), b. 1950. Her dance pieces have some similarities to Cunningham's, but she has developed her own individual style. *Relay* (1972), *Something to Tell* (1980), *Different Trains* (1990), *Trespass* (1996).

de Keersmaeker, Anna Teresa (Belgian), b. 1960. Began making repetitive, **abstract** dances to minimalist music, but her later work is more theatrical. *Bartók/Aantekeningen* (1986), *Achterland* (1990), *Drumming* (1998).

Duncan, Isadora (U.S.), 1877–1927. **Pioneer** of free dance; danced barefoot and in light clothes.

Dunham, Katherine (U.S.), 1909–2006. Successfully combined elements of modern, jazz, and Caribbean dance. *Barrelhouse* (1938), *Shango* (1946).

Forsythe, William (U.S.), b. 1949. Choreographer who has challenged the conventions of ballet with his own style of modern movement. *Artifact* (1984), *Impressing the Czar* (1988), *Endless House* (1999).

Fuller, Loie (U.S.), 1862–1928. Danced with skirts and lights. *Serpentine Dance* (1891), *The Butterfly* (1892), *Fire Dance* (1895).

Gades, Antonio (Spanish), b. 1936. Flamenco dancer who has incorporated some modern dance ideas into his work. *Blood Wedding* (1981).

Gordon, David (U.S.), b. 1936. Post-modern dancer and choreographer. His pieces often include film, popular music, and speech. *Field, Chair and Mountain* (1985).

Graham, Martha (U.S.), 1894–1991. One of the first and greatest modern dance pioneers. Made dramatic dance pieces and developed her own technique. *Lamentation* (1930), *Appalachian Spring* (1944), *Acrobats of God* (1960).

Halprin, Anna (U.S.), b. 1920. Dance improviser and teacher. Taught many post-modern dance pioneers.

Holm, Hanya (German-U.S.), 1893–1992. Trained with Mary Wigman, then opened a dance school in the United States. Trained many important dancers.

Humphrey, Doris (U.S.), 1895–1958. U.S. dance pioneer along with Graham. Made group pieces and some using abstract movement. *The Art of Making Dances* (1959), *The Shakers* (1931), *Passacaglia in C* (1938).

Jones, Bill T. (U.S.), b. 1952. Became famous for work with partner Arnie Zane in 1980s. Since Zane died in 1988 he has continued to make challenging dances. *Secret Pastures* (1984), *Still/Here* (1994).

Jooss, Kurt (German), 1901–1979. His dance company developed Laban's movement principles. *The Green Table* (1932) was a powerful anti-war dance.

Khan, Akram (British-Bangladeshi), b. 1974. Choreographer who has brought together modern and post-modern movements with Indian **kathak** dance. *Polaroid Feet* (2001), *kaash* (2002), *Sacred Monsters* (2006).

Kylián, Jiří (Czech), b. 1947. Director of Netherlands Dance Theater, whose work combines elements of ballet and modern dance. *Symphony of Psalms* (1978), *Forgotten Land* (1981), *Stamping Ground* (1983).

Laban, Rudolph (Hungarian), 1879–1958. His dance philosophy and teaching influenced many dancers. Dance notation system.

Lafrance, Noémie (Canadian), b. 1974. Choreographer who specializes in dances for specific places, such as *Descent* (2002) in a spiral stairwell, and *Noir* (2004) in a multi-story parking lot.

Limón, José (Mexican-U.S.), 1908–1972. Worked with Doris Humphrey, then set up his own company. Further developed Humphrey's dance technique. *The Moor's Pavane* (1949).

Lock, Édouard (Canadian), b. 1954. Formed company La La La Human Steps. His energetic, gymnastic dances are popular worldwide. Has worked with rock stars such as David Bowie. *Orange* (1981), *Human Sex* (1985).

Monk, Meredith (U.S.), b. 1942. Dancer, singer, and composer. Part of post-modern dance in 1960s; has continued to make "operas" combining performance, and music. *Juice* (1969), *Education of the Girlchild* (1973), *Turtle Dreams* (1983), *Magic Frequencies* (1998).

Morris, Mark (U.S.), b. 1956. One of greatest choreographers of recent years. Dances are extremely varied but always musical. *Gloria* (1981), *L'Allegro, il Penseroso ed il Moderato* (1988), *The Hard Nut* (1991), *Falling Down Stairs* (1997).

Newson, Lloyd (Australian), b. 1954. Director of DV8 Physical Theater, making dance pieces about the real world and involving the dancers in the making of the piece. *Dead Dreams of Monochrome Men* (1988), *Enter Achilles* (1995), *The Cost of Living* (2003).

Nikolais, Alwin (U.S.), 1910–1993. Pioneer of multimedia dance pieces, combining lighting effects, costumes, film, and movement. Worked closely with choreographer Murray Louis. *Kaleidoscope* (1953), *Grotto* (1973).

Paxton, Steve (U.S.), b. 1939. Pioneer of post-modern dance and contact **improvisation**.

Petronio, Stephen (U.S.), b. 1956. Danced with Trisha Brown before setting up his own company. Choreography is often about aggression and clashes of ideas. *Simulacrum Reels* (1987), *Wrong Wrong* (with Michael Clarke 1991).

Primus, Pearl (U.S.), 1919–1994. African-American choreographer who brought ideas from west African and Caribbean dance into her work. *Strange Fruit* (1943), *African Ceremonial* (1944).

Shawn, Ted (U.S.), 1891–1972. Formed Denishawn School with St. Denis. Formed first all-male modern dance group. *Kinetic Molpai* (1935).

Sokolow, Anna (U.S.), 1910–2000. Trained with Graham, choreographed many works on dark subjects such as the **Holocaust** and the Spanish Civil War. *Slaughter of the Innocents* (1934).

St. Denis, Ruth (U.S.), 1879–1968. Brought Eastern ideas into her dance, trained first modern dancers. *Radha* (1906), *Egypta* (1909), *O-Mika* (1913).

Tatsumi Hijikata (Japanese), 1928–1986. Developed butoh style of dance in late 1950s. *Kinjiki* ("Forbidden Colors," 1959).

Taylor, Paul (U.S.), b. 1930. One of the most accessible and successful of all modern dancers. Wide range of dances from experimental *Seven New Dances* (1957) to joyful *Esplanade* (1975).

Tharp, Twyla (U.S.), b. 1941. Mix of modern, jazz, ballet, and quirky humor has made her dance style popular worldwide. *Eight Jelly Rolls* (1971), *When Push Comes to Shove* (1976), *Catherine Wheel* (1981).

Ushio Amagatsu (Japanese), b. 1949. Brought butoh to worldwide audiences with his company, Sankai Juku. *Kinkan Shonen* ("The Kumquat Seed," 1978).

Vandekeybus, Wim (Belgian), b. 1964. His physical, high-impact choreography often involves film and drama as well as dance.

Weidman, Charles (U.S.), 1901–1975. Began a company with Doris Humphrey, then set up on his own. Used witty choreography. *And Daddy Was a Fireman Too* (1943).

Wigman, Mary (German), 1886–1973. Expressionist form of dance—expressed ideas and emotions through pure movement. *Witch Dance* (1914).

Glossary

abstract dance or other kind of art that does not tell a story or show the real world

arthritis joint disease that can damage joints and make movement painful

autism disorder in which a person finds it difficult to communicate and interact with other people

avant-garde new and experimental kinds of dance or other kinds of art

balletic movement that is like ballet

Baroque European art, music, and architecture from about the 17th and 18th centuries

canon piece of dance in which two dancers perform the same movements but start at different times

censorship not being allowed to write or talk about a subject

choreographer person who creates a dance

choreography art or skill of creating a dance

hand jive dance using only hand and arm gestures

Holocaust murder of millions of Jews by the Nazis during World War II

improvisation inventing something, such as a dance, on the spot

kathak kind of dance from north India involving rhythmic stamping and elaborate gestures

martial arts ancient methods of fighting from Japan and China that are now taught as sports

meditation method for relaxing and focusing the mind

Paris Exhibition large public exhibition with many events that happened in 1900

patron someone who supports artists with encouragement, help, and money

Pilates form of exercise that improves posture and concentration

pioneer someone who is the first to do something

promoter someone who arranges concerts and other performances

revue popular theater performance involving music, dancing, and comedy sketches

sacrifice kill an animal or human for religious reasons

special needs people who need special help with their education

Tai Chi type of movement training from China that was originally a martial art

therapy treatment of illness or disability

Further Information

Books

Bremser, Martha, and Deborah Jowitt. *Fifty Contemporary Choreographers: A Reference Guide*. New York: Routledge, 1999.

Brown, Jean Morrison. *The Vision of Modern Dance*. Hightstown, N.J.: Princeton Book Company, 1997.

Derezinski, Amelia. *Twyla Tharp*. New York: Rosen, 2005.

Escoffier, Jeffrey, and Matthew Lore. *Mark Morris' L'allegro, il Penseroso ed il Moderato*. New York: Marlowe, 2002.

Freedman, Russell. *Martha Graham, A Dancer's Life*. New York: Clarion, 1998.

Lihs, Harriet. *Appreciating Dance, A Guide to the World's Liveliest Art*. Hightstown, N.J.: Princeton Book Company, 2002.

Mazo, Joseph H. *Prime Movers, the Makers of Modern Dance in America*. Hightstown, N.J.: Princeton Book Company, 2000.

Tracy, Robert. *Ailey Spirit: The Journey of an American Dance Company*. New York: Stewart, Tabori & Chang, 2004.

Websites

Most dancers and dance companies have their own websites. There are also a lot of video clips of dance pieces on YouTube.

www.pbs.org/newshour/bb/entertainment/markmorris/primer.html
Basic information about U.S. modern dance from the Public Broadcasting Service. It includes video of Mark Morris's *Falling Down Stairs*.

www.artsalive.ca/en/dan/dance101/index.asp
Covers many different kinds of dance and provides an interactive guide to making dances.

http://artsedge.kennedy-center.org/marthagraham/index.htm
Learn the story of a dancer about to join the Martha Graham Dance Company.

http://digitalgallery.nypl.org/nypldigital/explore/dgexplorecfm?topic=arts&collection_list=DanceinPhotographsan&col_id=216
An excellent collection of early modern dance photos.

www.alvinailey.org
The website of the Alvin Ailey American Dance Theater.

www.merce.org
The website of the Merce Cunningham Dance Company.

www.marthagraham.org
The website of the Martha Graham Dance Company.

Index